A BEGINNER'S SONG BOOKLET

for the

16 String Lyre-Harp

Arranged by Melanie Allen

PREFACE

Looking for an instrument I could learn to play in my retirement, and always being especially fond of harp music, I decided to purchase a 16 string lyre-harp. I was so excited to open the box containing my lyre, a carrying case, a tuning tool, a pick, a cleaning cloth, and instructions which contained two songs: TWO songs! And what was worse, I couldn't make heads or tails of how to play them!

Of course, I could experiment and pick out tunes I knew well; but (as with age comes struggles with memory) I wanted a booklet of songs I could learn from and reference without the struggle of writing every note down myself, and I didn't want to pay a lot for them. Hunting around the internet, I found a few YouTube videos and some individual sheet music to print out but absolutely no inexpensive song booklets for the 16 string lyre. And, since I had no experience with a lyre or a harp (and very little proficiency reading music), individual songs I did find were like trying to decode hieroglyphs without the benefit of a Rosetta Stone.

To make a long story short, I decided to create my own 16 string lyre-harp song booklet for anyone else who, like me, wants to enjoy some simple tunes while learning to play.

The songs are arranged with three references:
The top line refers to each string (1-16) from left to right (facing you).
The middle refers to the actual notes on the musical staff.
The bottom refers to the scale of C in lyre notation.

In this booklet, you will find ten Classical and Folk Songs and twelve Christmas Songs; I hope they bring you pleasure.

Sincerely,

Melanie Allen

P.S. Please excuse any incorrect musical staff notations or inconsistencies which come from working with the free portion of an app that wouldn't allow me to edit without subscribing and paying.

Classical and Folk Songs

Amazing Grace

Hymn by E.O Excell and John Newton

(Can also be played an octave lower.)

Erie Canal

Thomas S. Allen

NOTE: * Tune String 10 (B4) to A4#

Happy Birthday

Traditional

(Can be played an octave lower starting on G3.)

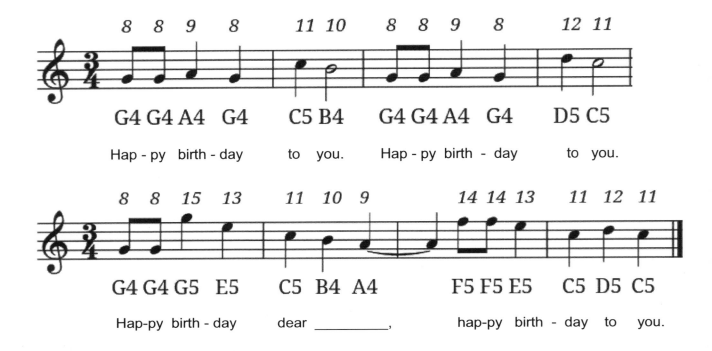

8 8 9 8   11 10   8 8 9 8   12 11

G4 G4 A4 G4   C5 B4   G4 G4 A4 G4   D5 C5

Hap - py birth - day   to you.   Hap - py birth - day   to you.

8 8 15 13   11 10 9   14 14 13   11 12 11

G4 G4 G5 E5   C5 B4 A4   F5 F5 E5   C5 D5 C5

Hap-py birth - day   dear _____,   hap-py birth - day to you.

Lullaby

Johannes Brahms

Ode to Joy

Ludwig von Beethoven

Scarborough Faire

Scottish Folk Tune

REPEAT AT REST IN LINE 1 TO END OF LINE 3.

Shenandoah

Old American Folk Song

1   4   4   4   4   5   6   7   9   8   11 10 9

G3 C4 C4 C4   C4 D4 E4 F4 A4 G4   C5 B4 A4

Oh, Shen - an - do - ah,   I   long   to   see   you.   A----- way,
Oh, Shen - an - do - ah,   I   love   your   daugh-ter.   A----- way,
Oh, Shen - an - do - ah,   I   long   to   hear   you.   Far a - way,

8   9   8   6   8   8   9   9   9   9   6   8   6   5

G4 A4 G4 E4   G4   G4   A4 A4   A4 A4   E4 G4 E4 D4

you roll - in' riv - ver.   Oh, Shen - an - do - ah,   I   long   to   see
you roll - in' riv - ver.   For   her, I'd   cross----- your roaring wat -
you roll - in' riv - ver.   Oh, Shen - an - do - ah,   just   to   be   near

4   5   6   4   6   9   8   4   4   5   6   4   5   4

C4   D4 E4   C4 E4 A4 G4   C4 C4 D4   E4   C4 D4   C4

you.   A - way. We're bound a - way.   A - cross the   wide Miss - ou - ri.
ers.   A - way. We're bound a - way.   A - cross the   wide Miss - ou - ri.
you.   Far away. We're far a - way.   A - cross the   wide Miss - ou - ri.

Shortnin' Bread

Traditional

Try a few easy chords.

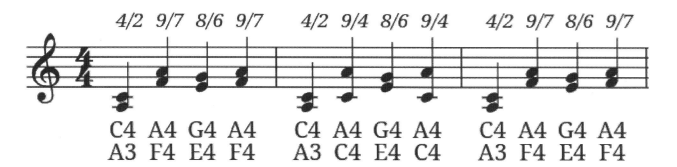

4/2 9/7 8/6 9/7   4/2 9/4 8/6 9/4   4/2 9/7 8/6 9/7

C4 A4 G4 A4   C4 A4 G4 A4   C4 A4 G4 A4
A3 F4 E4 F4   A3 C4 E4 C4   A3 F4 E4 F4

Momma's little baby loves   short-nin,, short-nin'; Momma's little baby loves

6/4 5/3 4/2   11 11   8   9   8   11   11 8   9   10

E4 D4 C4   C5 C5   G4 A4 G4   C5   C5 G4 A4 B4
C4 B3 A3

short-nin' bread.   Put on   the ket - tle,   Put   on   the tea, 'cause

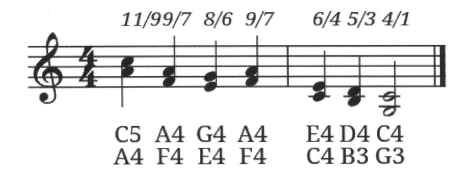

11/99/7 8/6 9/7   6/4 5/3 4/1

C5 A4 G4 A4   E4 D4 C4
A4 F4 E4 F4   C4 B3 G3

Momma's little baby loves   short-nin' bread.

Simple Gifts

Joseph Brackett

(Can be played an octave lower starting on G3.)

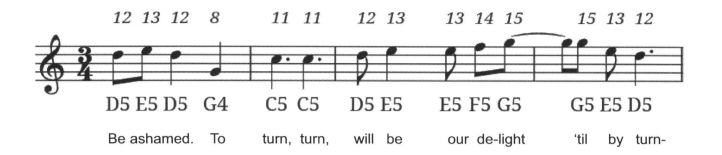

Taoist Love Theme, A

M. A. Martin

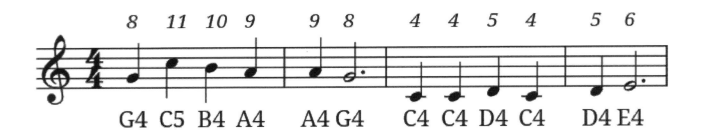

Christmas Songs

1. Deck the Halls

2. First Noel, The

3. God Rest Ye, Merry Gentlemen

4. Hark! The Herald Angels Sing

5. Jingle Bells

6. Joy to the World

7. O, Come All Ye Faithful

8. O, Holy Night

9   Silent Night

10. Sing for Peace and Love Ev'rywhere

11. We Three Kings

12. We Wish You a Merry Christmas

Deck the Halls

Traditional

First Noel, The

Traditional

God Rest Ye, Merry Gentlemen

Traditional

2 2 6   6 5 4   3 2 1   2 3 4   5 6

A3 A3 E4   E4 D4 C4   B3 A3 G3   A3 B3 C4   D4 E4

God rest ye,   mer-ry gen - tle men,   let   noth - ing you   dis-may.

2 2 6   6 5 4   3 2 1   2 3 4   5 6

A3 A3 E4   E4 D4 C4   B3 A3 G3   A3 B3 C4   D4 E4

Re - mem - ber   Christ our sav - i - or   was   born on Christ - mas day.

6 7 5   6 7 8   9 6 5   4 2 3   4 5

E4 F4 D4   E4 F4 G4   A4 E4 D4   C4 A3 B3   C4 D4

To   save us   all   from sa - tan's power when   we were   gone   a - stray.

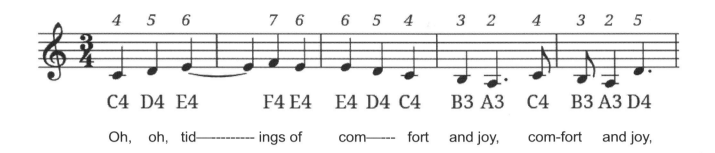

Oh, oh, tid——————— ings of   com——— fort   and joy,   com-fort   and joy,

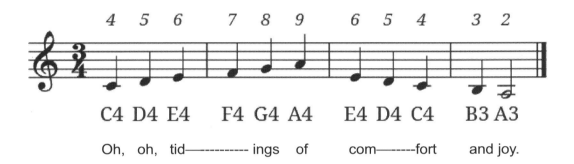

Oh, oh, tid————————— ings of   com———————fort   and joy.

Hark! The Herald Angels Sing

Music by Felix Mendelssohn
Words by Charles Wesley

Hark! The her - ald   an - gels sing —   Glor - y   to   the   new-born king.
Hail   the heaven born prince of peace —   Hail   the son   of   right-ous-ness!

Peace on earth,   and   mer - cy mild — ,   God and sin - ners   re - con - ciled.
Light and life   to   all   he   brings — ,   risen with heal - ing   in his wings.

Joy - ful all   ye   na - tions rise — ,   Join the triumph —   of   the   skies.
Mild he lays his   glor - y   by—---,   Born that man no   more my die — .

| 9 | 9 | 9 | 8 | 7 | 6 | 7 | 5 | 6 | 7 | 8 | 4 | 4 | 5 | 6 |

A4   A4 A4 G4   F4 E4 F4   D4 E4 F4 G4   C4   C4 D4 E4

WIth   an - gel - ic   host pro-claim.   Christ is —   born   in   Beth - le - hem.
Born   to   raise the sons of earth;   born   to —   give   them sec - ond birth.

| 9 | 9 | 9 | 8 | 7 | 6 | 7 | 5 | 6 | 7 | 8 | 4 | 4 | 5 | 4 |

A4   A4 A4 G4   F4 E4 F4   D4 E4 F4 G4   C4   C4 D4 C4

Hark!   The her - ald   an - gels sing!   Glory ——————— to   the   new-born king.
Hark!   The her - ald   an - gels sing!   Glory ——————— to   the   new-born king.

Jingle Bells

Traditional

Try some easy chords.

Joy to the World

Music by George Frideric Handel
Words by Issac Watts

O, Come All Ye Faithful

Traditional

C4 C4 G3 C4 D4 G3   E4 D4 E4 F4 E4 D4

Oh, come all ye faith - ful, joy-ful and tri - umph - ant;

C4 C4 B3 A3 B3 C4 D4 E4 B3 A3   G3 G3

oh, come ye oh, come — ye to Be - eth - le - hem.

G4 F4 E4 F4 E4 D4 E4 C4 D4 B3 A3 G3 C4

Come and be - hold him, born the king of a - angels. Oh,

come let us a - dore him. Oh, come let us a - dore him,

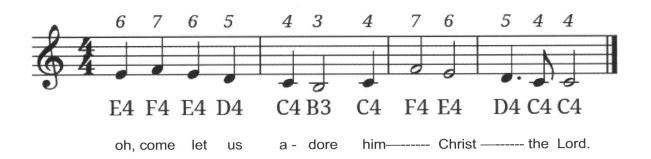

oh, come let us a - dore him——— Christ ——— the Lord.

O, Holy Night

Traditional

6 6 6 8 8 9 9 7 9 11 8 8 6 5

E4 E4 E4 G4 G4 A4 A4 F4 A4 C5 G4 G4 E4 D4

Oh, ho - ly night, the star are bright - ly shin - ing; it is the

4 6 7 8 7 5 4 6 6 6 8 8

C4 E4 F4 G4 F4 D4 C4 E4 E4 E4 G4 G4

night of our dear savior's birth. Long lay the world in

9 9 7 9 11 8 8 7 6 10 8 9

A4 A4 F4 A4 C5 G4 G4 F4 E4 B4 G4 A4

sin and er - ror pin - ing 'til he ap - peared and the

10 11 10 6 8 8 9 5 8 9 8 11 6 9

B4 C4 B4 E4 G4 G4 A4 D4 G4 A4 G4 C5 E4 A4

soul felt its worth. A thrill of hope the weary world re - joy -

28

Silent Night

Traditional

Sing for Peace and Love Ev'rywhere

M. A. Martin

We Three Kings

Traditional

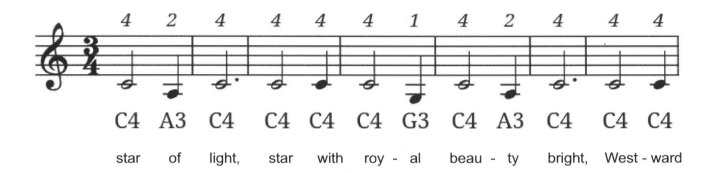

C4 A3 C4 C4 C4 C4 G3 C4 A3 C4 C4 C4

star of light, star with roy - al beau - ty bright, West - ward

D4 E4 F4 E4 D4 E4 C4 C4 C4 G3 C4 A3 C4

lead - ing still pro - ceed - ing, guide us to thy per - fect light.

We Wish You a Merry Christmas

Traditional

(Can also be played an octave lower - starting on the first string G3.)

Template for Creating Your Own Songs

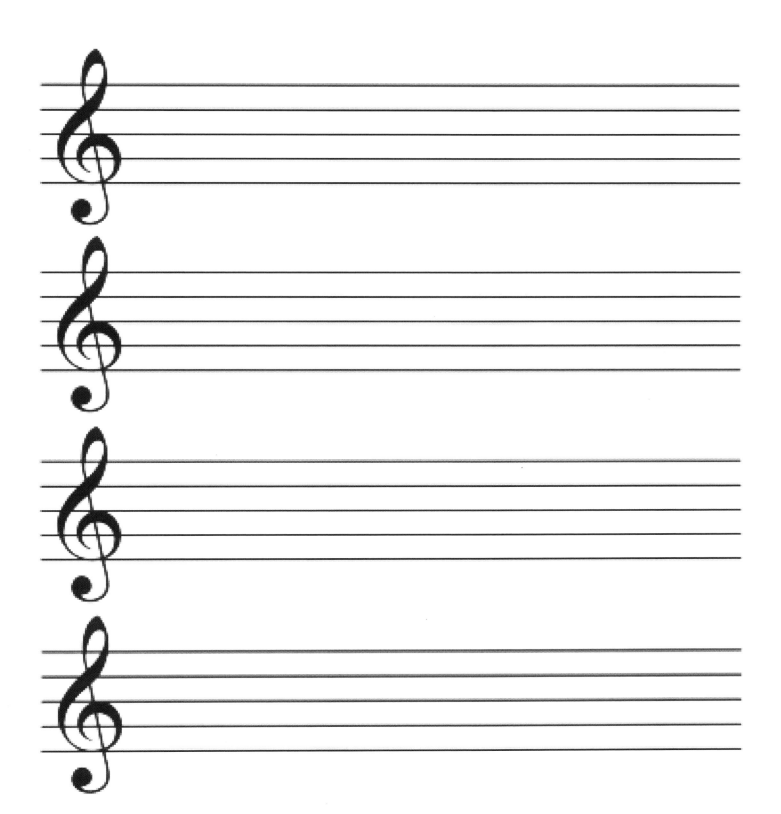

Printed in Great Britain
by Amazon